Perfect Iced Coffee

40 Recipes for Making Great Iced Coffee at Home

BY: Nancy Silverman

COPYRIGHT NOTICES

© 2019 Nancy Silverman All Rights Reserved

Subject to the agreement and permission of the author, this Book, in part or in whole, may not be reproduced in any format. This includes but is not limited to electronically, in print, scanning or photocopying.

The opinions, guidelines and suggestions written here are solely those of the Author and are for information purposes only. Every possible measure has been taken by the Author to ensure accuracy but let the Reader be advised that they assume all risk when following information. The Author does not assume any risk in the case of damages, personally or commercially, in the case of misinterpretation or misunderstanding while following any part of the Book.

My Heartfelt Thanks and A Special Reward for Your Purchase!

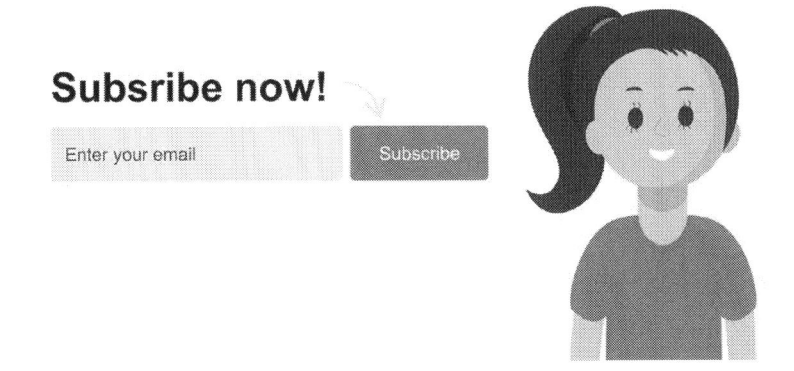

https://nancy.gr8.com

My heartfelt thanks at purchasing my book and I hope you enjoy it! As a special bonus, you will now be eligible to receive books absolutely free on a weekly basis! Get started by entering your email address in the box above to subscribe. A notification will be emailed to you of my free promotions, no purchase necessary! With little effort, you will be eligible for free and discounted books daily. In addition to this amazing gift, a reminder will be sent 1-2 days before the offer expires to remind you not to miss out. Enter now to start enjoying this special offer!

Table of Contents

(1) Vietnamese Iced Coffee 7

(2) Australian Maple Iced Coffee 9

(3) Viennese Iced Coffee 11

(4) Banana Latte 13

(5) Vanilla Bean Iced Latte 15

(6) Black Forest Iced Coffee 17

(7) Thai Iced Coffee Recipe 19

(8) Boozy Iced Coffee 21

(9) Swedish Iced Coffee Lemonade 23

(10) Churro Iced Coffee Float 25

(11) Strawberry Dream Iced Coffee 28

(12) Cinnamon Cream Upside Down Vanilla Iced Coffee 30

(13) Spiked Iced Coffee 32

(14) Coco Almond Mocha Macchiato 34

(15) Spanish Iced Coffee 36

(16) Coconut Iced Coffee 38

(17) Skinny Caramel Frappuccino 40

(18) Coconut Water Ice Coffee 42

(19) Salted Chocolate Iced Coffee 44

(20) Coffee Colada Iced Coffee 46

(21) Salted Caramel Ice Coffee 48

(22) Cookies n Crème Mocha 51

(23) Raspberry Frappe 53

(24) Dark Italian Iced Coffee 55

(25) Portuguese (Mazagran) Iced Coffee 57

(26) Date and Vanilla Iced Coffee 59

(27) Peppermint Iced Mocha... 61

(28) East Meets West 63

(29) PB & C Frappuccino 65

(30) English Toffee Iced Latte 67

Perfect Iced Coffee - 5

(31) Morning Iced Coffee 69

(32) French Vanilla Iced Coffee 71

(33) Limerick Latte Ice Coffee 73

(34) German Iced Coffee 75

(35) Indian Coffee Lassi 77

(36) Greek Frappé 79

(37) Iced S'mores Latte 81

(38) Hazelnut Iced Coffee 83

(39) Iced Cappuccino 85

(40) Iced Almond Macadamia Latte 87

About the Author 89

Author's Afterthoughts 91

(1) Vietnamese Iced Coffee

Vietnamese iced coffee, is also known as Cà Phê đá. This version is a traditional recipe.

Yield: 4

Preparation Time: 10mins

Ingredient List:

- 4 cups water
- ½ cup dark roast coffee
- ½ cup sweetened condensed milk
- 16 ice cubes

Instructions:

Brew the coffee in your preferred way. Add 2 tablespoons of condensed milk into each of the 4 coffee glasses. Pour 1 cup of hot coffee into each and stir well to dissolve.

Add 4 ice cubes to each of the tall glasses. Pour the hot coffee over the cubes and stir well, using a long-stemmed spoon.

(2) Australian Maple Iced Coffee

Down Under they like their iced coffee sweet, syrupy and made with ice cream. Be warned though, it's addictive.

Yield: 1

Preparation Time:2mins

Ingredient List:

- 2 small scoops vanilla ice cream
- ¾ cup brewed coffee (cold)
- Maple syrup
- Splash whole milk
- Whipped cream
- Chocolate shavings

Instructions:

Scoop the vanilla ice cream into a tall glass. Top with the cold brewed coffee. Add maple syrup, a little at a time, to taste. Add a splash of milk.

Top with whipped cream and scatter with dark chocolate shavings.

(3) Viennese Iced Coffee

Serve with almond biscotti as a perfect end to a dinner party.

Yield: 4

Preparation Time:15mins

Ingredient List:

- 6 (1 ounce) shots espresso
- 3 tbsp. sugar
- 1 tsp vanilla extract
- ¼ cup hot water
- 2 cups ice
- 4 scoops coffee ice cream
- Cocoa powder (unsweetened)

Instructions:

Using a food blender combine the espresso shots, sugar, vanilla extract and hot water. Blitz until the sugar has dissolved. Add the ice to the blender and blend until silky. Divide the coffee mixture evenly between 4 short glasses.

Add the ice cream to a microwave safe bowl, and microwave on a high setting for 10-15 seconds, or until soft but not liquid.

Scoop one ball of melted ice cream into each of the 4 glasses. Using a fine sifter, sprinkle cocoa powder on top of the ice cream.

Serve with a short straw.

(4) Banana Latte

You can make iced coffee with virtually any flavored syrup in the store cupboard.

Yield: 1

Preparation Time: 2mins

Ingredient List:

- Ice
- ½ cup strong brewed coffee (chilled)
- 1 cup whole milk
- 2½ tbsp. banana syrup

IIIIIIIIIIIIIIIIIIIIIIIIIIIIIIIIIIIIIIIIIIIIIIIIII

Instructions:

In a tall glass filled with ice add the coffee, whole milk and syrup. Stir well to combine.

(5) Vanilla Bean Iced Latte

Fresh vanilla beans give an intense and smooth flavor that you don't get with vanilla essence.

Yield: 1

Preparation Time:20mins

Ingredient List:

- 1 cup strong brewed coffee (warm)
- ¼ cup coconut milk
- 1½ tsp pure maple syrup
- ¼ tsp fresh vanilla beans
- ⅛ tsp cinnamon

Instructions:

Add the brewed coffee, milk, maple syrup, vanilla beans and cinnamon to a cup. Allow to stand at room temperature for a quarter of an hour.

Pour into a tall glass and fill with ice. Serve immediately!

(6) Black Forest Iced Coffee

Who needs gateaux when you can enjoy the flavors of cherry and chocolate in a tall glass?

Yield: 1

Preparation Time:3mins

Ingredient List:

- 1 shot espresso (chilled)
- 6 ounces chocolate milk
- 2 cups ice
- 1 tbsp. cherry syrup
- 1 tbsp. almond syrup

Instructions:

Combine the espresso, milk, ice and syrups in a food blender and blitz until silky.

Serve in a tall glass.

(7) Thai Iced Coffee Recipe

An iced coffee for all you hardened caffeine drinkers out there.

Yield: 3-4

Preparation Time: 24hours 10mins

Ingredient List:

- 4 tbsp. ground dark double espresso
- 12 ounces purified water
- 4 ounces cashew milk
- 1 tsp ground cardamom
- 1 tsp cinnamon
- ¼ tsp nutmeg
- 2 tbsp. raw sugar
- 1 tbsp. coconut cream
- ½ tsp vanilla extract

Instructions:

First, using a French press, brew the coffee. Add the espresso to the press, as well as the hot water, press down and allow to stand for 4-5 minutes.

Meanwhile, in a large heatproof jug, mix the cashew milk with the spices, sugar, coconut cream and vanilla extract.

Pour the coffee from the French press into the mixture. Stir well, and when slightly cooled transfer to the refrigerator for 24 hours. This process will ensure that the flavors have time to infuse.

(8) Boozy Iced Coffee

An alcoholic iced coffee packed full of sweet, nutty flavors.

Yield: 1

Preparation Time: 8hours 2mins

Ingredient List:

- 6 ounces strong brewed coffee, well-chilled
- 4 ice cubes
- 1-ounce hazelnut liqueur
- 1 ounce half-and-half
- Sweetener (of choice)
- Whipped coconut cream
- ½ tsp dark chocolate shavings
- ½ tsp chocolate syrup

Instructions:

Brew the coffee in your preferred way. Allow the coffee to cool. When cool, pour the coffee into a large jug and place in the refrigerator until chilled, for at least 6-8 hours.

Add ice cubes to a tall glass and pour the chilled mixture on top. Add the hazelnut liqueur, half and half, and your sweetener of choice. Stir well to thoroughly combine the ingredients.

Serve. Alternatively, garnish with coconut cream, chocolate shavings and a dash of chocolate syrup.

(9) Swedish Iced Coffee Lemonade

Kaffelemonad from Sweden is a refreshing change from standard iced coffees. A variation of Portuguese Mazagran.

Yield: 2

Preparation Time:20mins

Ingredient List:

Lemon syrup;

- 1 cup organic cane sugar
- 1 cup cold water
- Zest of 1 lemon

Ice Coffee Lemonade

- 3 parts brewed coffee
- 2 parts freshly squeezed lemon juice
- 1 part lemon syrup
- 2 parts tonic water
- Ice cubes

Instructions:

For the lemon syrup: In a saucepan, combine the cane sugar with the water and zest. Heat over medium temperature. Stir constantly until all of the sugar has dissolved. Remove from the heat. Set aside to to cool. When the syrup is cool, transfer to the refrigerator.

For the iced coffee lemonade: In a cocktail shaker combine all 5 ingredients and shake vigorously. Serve.

(10) Churro Iced Coffee Float

Creamy ice cream combines with spicy cinnamon and a shot of espresso to bring you coffee and dessert in one tall glass.

Yield: 1

Preparation Time: 25mins

Ingredient List:

- ½ can sweetened condensed milk
- ½ cup half and half
- 4 cinnamon sticks
- Dash of vanilla extract
- 2 shots espresso
- Ice cubes
- Cream soda (cold)
- Vanilla ice cream
- Cinnamon sugar

Instructions:

In a saucepan over low heat, add the condensed milk to the half and half and cinnamon sticks.

Cook for 7-8 minutes while the cinnamon infuses. Remove from the heat, add the vanilla extract. Discard the cinnamon sticks and pour the mixture into a heat proof jar. Transfer the creamer to the refreigerator where it will keep for up to 7 days.

Pour the espresso shot into a tall coffee glass, add the ice cubes along with the churro cramer, and top up with cold cream soda.

Garnish with a generous scoop of ice cream and sprinkle with a little cinnamon sugar.

(11) Strawberry Dream Iced Coffee

Strawberries and cream are already a winning combination, add coffee and you'll have a decadent new way to get your caffeine fix.

Yield: 1

Preparation Time: 5mins

Ingredient List:

- 8 ice cubes
- ½ cup strong brewed coffee (cool)
- ⅓ cup strawberry puree
- 1½ tbsp. heavy cream

Instructions:

Add the ice cubes to a cocktail mixer. Pour in the remaining ingredients and shake for 30-60 seconds to combine.

Strain into a tall glass filled with ice and serve immediately.

(12) Cinnamon Cream Upside Down Vanilla Iced Coffee

This iced coffee may sound complicated but it's actually super easy!

Yield: 1

Preparation Time: 20mins

Ingredient List:

- ½ cup whipped topping
- ½ tsp ground cinnamon
- ¾ cup store bought vanilla ice coffee

Instructions:

In a small bowl, whisk together the whipped topping and cinnamon until combined.

Spoon into the bottom of a medium-large glass and place upright in the freezer for a quarter of an hour.

Pour the vanilla iced coffee slowly over top and serve immediately!

(13) Spiked Iced Coffee

Coffee spiked with coffee liqueur. A luxurious drink for those special times with your significant other.

Yield: 2

Preparation Time:10mins

Ingredient List:

- 4 tbsp. sweetened condensed milk
- 2 cups strong coffee, cool
- 2 ounces coffee liqueur
- Ice cubes

Instructions:

Divide the condensed milk evenly between 2 highball glasses. Add the cooled coffee and coffee liqueur. Stir well. Add ice and enjoy.

(14) Coco Almond Mocha Macchiato

A winning combination of all our favorite things; strong coffee, vanilla, coconut, almond and chocolate.

Yield: 2

Preparation Time:5mins

Ingredient List:

- 2 tbsp. chocolate syrup
- 1 double shot espresso (chilled)
- ½ cup vanilla flavored coconut milk
- 1 tbsp. almond and vanilla flavored creamer
- 1 tbsp. coconut sugar

Instructions:

Drizzle chocolate syrup inside of a tall glass. Fill with ice.

In a separate cup combine the vanilla coconut milk, almond vanilla creamer and coconut sugar. Stir well until the sugar dissolves. Pour slowly into the iced glass.

Slowly pour the espresso over top and serve immediately!

(15) Spanish Iced Coffee

A coffee typically enjoyed throughout Spain. Super strong and super sweet.

Yield: 6-8

Preparation Time: 1hour 10mins

Ingredient List:

- 4 cups super strong coffee (hot)
- ¼ cup condensed milk
- Seeds from 6 cardamom pods
- 2 cups whole fresh milk
- Ice cubes

Instructions:

Add the hot strong coffee and the condensed milk to a serving jug. Stir well to combine. Add the seeds from the cardamom pods and allow the coffee to cool.

Once cold, remove the seeds and pour in the whole milk. Transfer the jug to the refrigerator until the coffee is cold.

Serve, poured over ice cubes.

(16) Coconut Iced Coffee

Creamy coconut and strong coffee are the perfect combination for a sweet, creamy iced coffee.

Yield: 1-2

Preparation Time:5mins

Ingredient List:

- 1 cup canned unsweetened coconut milk (chilled)
- 1 cup brewed strong coffee (cold)
- 3 tbsp. chocolate syrup
- Ice cubes

Instructions:

Combine the coconut milk, cold coffee and syrup. Stir well to thoroughly combine.

Pour over ice and serve.

(17) Skinny Caramel Frappuccino

Guilt free, gluten free. At only 50 calories per serving you too can enjoy a coffee shop iced coffee without breaking the bank or your diet.

Yield: 2

Preparation Time: 2mins

Ingredient List:

- 3 cups ice cubes
- 1 cup brewed strong coffee (chilled)
- ½ cup unsweetened vanilla almond milk
- Sugar-free sweetener of choice
- ½ tsp vanilla extract
- 2 tbsp. fat- free whipped topping
- 1 tbsp. sugar-free caramel sauce

Instructions:

Add the ice cubes, coffee, vanilla almond milk, sweetener and vanilla extract to a food blender and blitz until frothy, this will take 1-2 minutes. Taste and adjust the flavoring accordingly. Add a little more coffee, milk, sweetener or ice cubes.

Pour into 2 tall glasses and garnish with fat-free whipped topping and a drizzle of caramel sauce.

Enjoy.

(18) Coconut Water Ice Coffee

Just three ingredients are all you'll need to make this refreshing iced coffee. Not only that, but coconut water is packed with electrolytes, making it a great option for a post workout pick me up or even a nasty hangover!

Yield: 1

Preparation Time:3mins

Ingredient List:

- 1 cup any brand coconut water
- ½ cup cold brew coffee concentrate
- Coconut flavored creamer

Instructions:

Combine the coconut water and cold brew concentrate in a tall glass and top with ice.

Pour a little coconut creamer over the top but don't stir.

Serve immediately!

(19) Salted Chocolate Iced Coffee

You must have tried salted caramel, but have you ever tried salted chocolate!? It may even be our new favorite thing.

Yield: 2

Preparation Time:5mins

Ingredient List:

- ½ cup whole milk
- 1 cup strong brewed coffee (room temperature)
- 2 tsp sweetened cocoa powder
- 6 drops stevia
- 1 scoop chocolate flavored protein
- ½ tsp sea salt

Instructions:

Add all ingredients into a blender and blitz until smooth.

Pour into two glasses and top with plenty of ice. Serve immediately!

(20) Coffee Colada Iced Coffee

High in taste and protein, low in fat and fuss.

Yield: 2

Preparation Time:10mins

Ingredient List:

- 2 ounces espresso
- 1 cup 1% milk
- 5 ounces piña colada coffee syrup
- 1 scoop vanilla protein powder

||||||||||||||||||||||||||||||||||||||||||||||||||

Instructions:

Brew the coffee in your preferred way. Pour the coffee over ice in order to cool it down quickly. Add the milk and piña colada syrup.

Transfer the mixture to a food blender and blitz until silky.

(21) Salted Caramel Ice Coffee

Make this coffee house favorite for your friends and family. Great for a coffee morning or get together.

Yield: 5

Preparation Time:25mins

Ingredient List:

- 1 cup granulated sugar
- ¼ cup cold water
- ¾ cup heavy cream
- 3 tbsp. salted butter
- ½ tsp fine sea salt
- ½ tsp vanilla extract
- 6 cups strong coffee

Instructions:

To make the caramel: In a heavy saucepan combine the granulated sugar with the water. Over medium heat, stir until the sugar has completely dissolved and is just beginning to come to a boil. Reduce the heat to medium-low. Continue to boil (without stirring) until the caramel sauce turns into a rich amber color, this will take around 8-10 minutes.

As soon as the sauce is a rich amber, remove the pan from the heat. Do this very quickly as the mixture is likely to burn. Add the heavy cream and whisk until silky. In the event of any clumps forming due to the inclusion of the cold cream, return the pan to a low heat and whisk until dissolved. Next add the butter, sea salt and vanilla extract.

Set the caramel sauce to one side to cool and thicken.

To make the caramel iced coffee: Put 2 tablespoons of the salted caramel sauce into each of the 5 coffee mugs. Add approximately 8 ounces of strong coffee and stir until the caramel has completely dissolved.

Take 5 separate glasses and fill with ice cubes. Pour the coffee-caramel mixture over the cubes of ice. Serve, adding a dash of milk, and a pinch of salt.

(22) Cookies n Crème Mocha

Ice cream makes for a super thick and creamy drink. Think iced coffee-milkshake hybrid.

Yield: 1-2

Preparation Time: 5mins

Ingredient List:

- 2 scoops cookies n crème ice cream
- ½ cup iced mocha coffee
- Whipped cream (for topping)
- 2 cookie n crème sandwich biscuits (crushed, for topping)

Instructions:

Add the ice cream and iced mocha coffee to a blender. Blitz until smooth.

Pour into a tall glass and swirl whipped cream on top. Sprinkle over the crushed cookies and serve!

(23) Raspberry Frappe

Raspberry flavorings work surprisingly well blended with strong coffee. Perfect on a hot day.

Yield: 1

Preparation Time:2mins

Ingredient List:

- ½ ounce raspberry syrup
- 3½ ounces whole milk
- 2 shots espresso (chilled)
- 2 cups ice

Instructions:

In a food blender combine all 4 ingredients and blitz until silky.

Serve with a long straw.

(24) Dark Italian Iced Coffee

The Italian stallion of iced beverages – strong, dark and tall.

Yield: 1

Preparation Time: 2mins

Ingredient List:

- 1 cup dark Italian roast coffee (chilled)
- 1 cup whole milk
- 3 tbsp. chocolate syrup
- ½ cup ice
- Whipped cream

Instructions:

In a small jug add the coffee, milk and syrup together. Add ice to a tall glass and pour the coffee-syrup mixture over the top.

Top with whipped cream.

(25) Portuguese (Mazagran) Iced Coffee

Mazagran originated in Algeria. This Portuguese version uses strong coffee, lemon juice and vanilla. The flavors fuse together to give you a great pick me up, any time of the day or night.

Yield: 1

Preparation Time: 30mins

Ingredient List:

- 2 tbsp. lemon juice
- 2 tbsp. simple syrup
- 3 tbsp. cold water
- 3-4 ice cubes
- 1 cup strong coffee (cold)
- ⅛ tsp vanilla extract

Instructions:

In a tall glass, combine the lemon juice, syrup and 3 tablespoons of cold water. Stir well to combine. Next add 3-4 ice cubes along with the coffee and vanilla extract, and blend. Transfer to the refrigerator to chill.

When chilled adjust the flavoring by adding lemon juice or syrup.

(26) Date and Vanilla Iced Coffee

Dates are a natural sweetener and give a malty, almost chocolatey flavor. They're a great alternative to chemical packed artificial 'low-cal' add-ins.

Yield: 1-2

Preparation Time:5mins

Ingredient List:

- 1 cup strong brewed coffee (chilled)
- 1½ cups vanilla almond milk
- ½ cup medjool dates (pitted, chopped)
- ½ tsp vanilla
- 1 cup ice
- ⅛ tsp sea salt

Instructions:

Add all ingredients into a blender and blitz until smooth.

Pour into your favorite glass and serve immediately!

(27) Peppermint Iced Mocha

A perfect choice for the holidays.

Yield: 1-2

Preparation Time:10mins

Ingredient List:

- 8 ounces strong brewed coffee
- 8 ounces chocolate milk (hot and steaming)
- 1-ounce peppermint syrup
- Chocolate syrup
- Ice cubes
- Whipped cream
- Peppermint candies (crushed)

Instructions:

In a microwave safe container, heat the chocolate milk until hot, but do not allow to boil. Next, add the hot coffee and peppermint syrup to the hot milk and stir well to combine. Put to one side to cool.

In a large glass, add the chocolate syrup, and ice cubes. Next pour in the cooled peppermint mocha and top with whipped cream topping and crushed peppermint candies.

(28) East Meets West

A popular beverage in Hong Kong. A mixture of the sweet milky tea and strong, but not bitter, coffee.

Yield: 1

Preparation Time: 2mins

Ingredient List:

- 1 cup of strong black tea (cold)
- 2 tsp simple syrup
- ⅓ cup of strong coffee (cold)
- 2 tbsp. whole milk
- Ice cubes

Instructions:

In a tall glass, combine the tea and simple syrup. Stir well. Next ad the cold coffee, whole milk and ice cubes. Stir well to combine.

Serve.

(29) PB & C Frappuccino

PB & C? Peanut butter and chocolate! Blended with a healthy dose of strong coffee this is the ultimate treat for hot summer days.

Yield: 1-2

Preparation Time: 5mins

Ingredient List:

- ¾ cup strong brewed coffee (cold)
- ½ cup skimmed milk
- 1 tbsp. Dutch processed cocoa powder
- 1 tbsp. peanut butter powder
- 2 cups ice
- Few drops stevia
- ½ tsp smooth peanut butter

Instructions:

Add all ingredients into a blender and blitz until smooth.

Pour into your favorite glass.

Warm the smooth peanut butter in the microwave and then drizzle over the Frappuccino.

Serve immediately!

(30) English Toffee Iced Latte

Toffee is an all-time favorite British candy. This recipe combines sweet toffee with strong coffee.

Yield: 1

Preparation Time:2mins

Ingredient List:

- 2½ tsp English toffee syrup
- 1 cup whole milk
- ½ cup strong brewed coffee (chilled)

Instructions:

In a tall glass filled with ice combine the 3 ingredients. Stir well and enjoy.

(31) Morning Iced Coffee

Nothing says Good Morning quite like a good cup of iced coffee.

Yield: 1

Preparation Time:8hours 10mins

Ingredient List:

- 10 ounces brewed coffee (refrigerated)
- 4 ounces brewed coffee
- Coffee ice cubes
- ½ ounce vanilla flavored syrup
- ⅓ cup milk

Instructions:

Using your coffee maker of choice, brew 10 ounces of coffee. Transfer to the refrigerator until cooled, ideally overnight.

Brew an additional 4 ounces of coffee. Allow to cool before pouring into an ice cube tray and freezing overnight.

When you are ready prepare your coffee, add the flavored ice cubes to a tall glass. Pour the cold coffee over the coffee ice cubes. Next, pour the vanilla syrup and milk. Stir well and savor the flavor.

(32) French Vanilla Iced Coffee

Ooh la la. Enjoy iced coffee Parisian style.

Yield: 1

Preparation Time: 2mins

Ingredient List:

- Ice
- 1 cup brewed coffee (chilled)
- 1-ounce French vanilla syrup
- Cream

Instructions:

Fill a tall glass with ice. Pour the chilled coffee and French syrup on top of the ice and top up with cream to taste.

(33) Limerick Latte Ice Coffee

Direct from the old country, an Irish, cream-infused iced coffee.

Yield: 1

Preparation Time: 5mins

Ingredient List:

- ¾ cup cola
- ¼ cup espresso (chilled)
- ¼ cup Irish cream syrup
- ¼ cup half and half
- ¼ tsp cinnamon

Instructions:

Fill a 16-ounce, tall glass half full with ice. Add the 6 ingredients and stir well to combine.

Sprinkle with ground cinnamon.

(34) German Iced Coffee

Enjoyed in many Mediterranean countries as a drink, this recipe can also be served as a dessert.

Yield: 1

Preparation Time:3mins

Ingredient List:

- 1 large scoop vanilla ice cream
- 1 cup strong coffee to taste (cold)
- Whipped cream (lightly sweetened)
- Dark chocolate (grated)

Instructions:

Spoon the ice cream into a tall glass. Pour the coffee over the top and add a dollop of whipped cream. Scatter with grated chocolate.

2. Serve with a straw.

(35) Indian Coffee Lassi

A creamy drink straight from India that uses yoghurt to make a thick cold coffee that can be enjoyed even as a light breakfast.

Yield: 2

Preparation Time: 5mins

Ingredient List:

- ⅓ cup espresso (cooled)
- ½ cup yoghurt
- 3 tbsp. sugar water (50/50 mix of water and sugar)
- 5 ice cubes

Instructions:

Add all ingredients into a blender and blitz until smooth.

Pour into two small glasses and serve.

(36) Greek Frappé

Enjoyed all over Greece, particularly during the hot summer, this iced frappé is a classic.

Yield: 1

Preparation Time: 3mins

Ingredient List:

- 2 tsp espresso powder or instant coffee
- 2 tsp sugar
- Cold water
- Ice cubes
- Milk

Instructions:

In a metal measuring cup, combine the espresso, sugar and 3 tablespoons of cold water.

Using an immersion or wand blender, mix until a thick foam begins to form, this will take 45-90 seconds.

Fill a tall glass with ice cubes and pour the foam over the ice cubes. Next, add up to 1 cup of cold water and milk. The foam will rise to the top. Drink using a straw.

(37) Iced S'mores Latte

You'll definitely want s'more after you taste this delicious cool coffee!

Yield: 1

Preparation Time:15mins

Ingredient List:

- ½ cup strong brewed coffee (hot)
- ¼ cup marshmallow fluff
- ½ cup whole milk
- 1 tbsp. chocolate syrup
- ½ tbsp. brown sugar

Instructions:

Add the hot coffee and marshmallow fluff to a blender. Blitz until totally combined.

Add in the milk, syrup and sugar, and blitz again.

Pour into a cocktail mixer and add in plenty of ice. Shake for 30-60 seconds to cool the coffee.

Strain the latte into a tall glass filled with ice and serve immediately!

(38) Hazelnut Iced Coffee

A nutty, chocolatey iced coffee; ideal for elevenses.

Yield: 2

Preparation Time: 9mins

Ingredient List:

- 2 tsp instant coffee powder
- 3 cups whole milk
- 1 tsp sugar
- 4 tbsp. hazelnut chocolate spread
- ½ tsp vanilla extract
- 12 ice cubes

Instructions:

In a food blender combine the first 5 ingredients. Blitz until frothy.

Add ice cubes to 2 tall glasses and pour the hazelnut coffee over the ice and stir.

(39) Iced Cappuccino

The secret to this indulgent creamy iced capp? Chocolate milk!

Yield: 1

Preparation Time: 5mins

Ingredient List:

- ⅛ cup boiling water
- 2 tbsp. powdered instant coffee
- 9 ice cubes
- 1½ tbsp. white sugar
- ½ cup chocolate milk
- ¼ cup cream

Instructions:

Pour the boiling water into a cup, and add in the coffee. Stir until the coffee dissolves and then pour into a blender.

Toss in the ice cubes, sugar and chocolate milk. Blitz until a frothy top forms. Add in the cream and blitz again until combined.

Serve in your favorite glass!

(40) Iced Almond Macadamia Latte

Nuts and dates combine perfectly with strong espresso coffee served over ice.

Yield: 1

Preparation Time: 8hours 10mins

Ingredient List:

- 1 cup blanched almonds
- ½ cup macadamia nuts
- ⅓ cup dates (pitted)
- 1 quart of filtered cold water
- 2 shots espresso (hot)
- Ice

Instructions:

In a large, plastic, lidded container, combine the first 3 ingredients. Add the filtered water to cover the mixture and allow to soak at room temperature, overnight.

In a food blender, on high speed, blitz until the mixture is a fine purée.

Using a fine mesh sieve resting over a bowl with 2 layers of fine cheesecloth, strain the mixture. The nut milk should be creamy and silky. Shake before use.

To make the latte: Using a cocktail shaker, combine 8 ounces of chilled nut milk, 2 shots of espresso, along with a few ice cubes. Shake it for about 40 seconds, then strain the liquid into a chilled glass.

About the Author

Nancy Silverman is an accomplished chef from Essex, Vermont. Armed with her degree in Nutrition and Food Sciences from the University of Vermont, Nancy has excelled at creating e-books that contain healthy and delicious meals that anyone can make and everyone can enjoy. She improved her cooking skills at the New England Culinary Institute in Montpelier Vermont and she has been working at perfecting her culinary style since graduation. She claims that her life's work is always a work in progress and she only hopes to be an inspiration to aspiring chefs everywhere.

Her greatest joy is cooking in her modern kitchen with her family and creating inspiring and delicious meals. She often says that she has perfected her signature dishes based on her family's critique of each and every one.

Nancy has her own catering company and has also been fortunate enough to be head chef at some of Vermont's most exclusive restaurants. When a friend suggested she share some of her outstanding signature dishes, she decided to add cookbook author to her repertoire of personal achievements. Being a technological savvy woman, she felt the e-book realm would be a better fit and soon she had her first cookbook available online. As of today, Nancy has sold over 1,000 e-books and has shared her culinary experiences and brilliant recipes with people from all over the world! She plans on expanding into self-help books and dietary cookbooks, so stayed tuned!

Author's Afterthoughts

Thank you for making the decision to invest in one of my cookbooks! I cherish all my readers and hope you find joy in preparing these meals as I have.

There are so many books available and I am truly grateful that you decided to buy this one and follow it from beginning to end.

I love hearing from my readers on what they thought of this book and any value they received from reading it. As a personal favor, I would appreciate any feedback you can give in the form of a review on Amazon and please be honest! This kind of support will help others make an informed choice on and will help me tremendously in producing the best quality books possible.

My most heartfelt thanks,

Nancy Silverman

If you're interested in more of my books, be sure to follow my author page on Amazon (can be found on the link Bellow) or scan the QR-Code.

https://www.amazon.com/author/nancy-silverman

Printed in Great Britain
by Amazon